MY
GRANDCHILDREN'S
AMERICA

Will it still be
the land of the free
and the home of the brave?

Don Jans

smea publishing

ISBN

978-0-615-60883-9

Copyright – pending
2012

First Edition

SMEA publishing

ACKNOWLEDGMENTS

I could not and would not have written this book if it were not for my daughter and son. While I was formulating my thoughts and ideas, my son was helpful and necessary to act as a sounding board. I wish to thank him for not only his patience, but also his insight, thoughts, and ideas. After I had my first draft on paper, I would not have continued if it were not for my daughter. She was the first person to read the initial transcript, and it was her honest and enthusiastic response that told me I should continue. Thank you both very much.

I also have to thank my grandchildren for the inspiration they were in my coming up with the idea to write and then continue through the many ups and downs. It was my oldest grandchild's insight and suggestions that led to the title. I look at those kids and hope they have the opportunity to live in a country that allows them to succeed or fail based on their ability, desire, and effort. Based on what I have seen from them so far, I know they will do very well, given the opportunity.

I also wish to thank my sister and her family, and my brother and his family, for indulging me and reading the initial transcripts and giving me honest feedback. It was very important and helpful. In addition, thank you Denise and Denny for taking the time to edit and correct. Also, thank you son for your editing, and thank you daughter for your designing and formatting. And, thank you grandkids for being so kind and cooperative to pose for the picture on the cover.

This was a concerted effort by my family and some friends. If I have missed anyone, I am sorry, it was not intentional.

PREFACE

You and I listen to the news and we read articles about the state of America. What we hear is very confusing and many times misleading. America has been a unique society that has offered unlimited opportunity for those who have had the ability and desire to achieve the goals they set for themselves. People who strived to achieve have been admired. Is this changing?

The accusations that some political leaders are employing communist or socialist ideals have become more common. In addition, current political leaders are also being called Marxist, or being compared to Karl Marx. I have been interested (people who know me say obsessed) in history and historical figures, including the life, times, and teachings of Karl Marx. It became increasingly clear to me that these accusations were not accurate and they were misleading. This was true of both the accuser and defender. In some cases this appeared to be intentional. In others it seemed to be because of not knowing the facts. I began to ask different people to tell me what they understood these concepts to mean. Most understandings were based on innuendo and not facts.

When people were told the facts, in a straightforward manner, they understood and were very interested in what has taken place in America and what is currently happening. We, as Americans, have been taught to be independent and think for ourselves. All we ask is that the facts be presented to us, simply and honestly.

Many of the people, with whom I had this discussion, encouraged me to write a book so all independent thinking Americans would have the facts, and be able to discern for themselves the wisdom or fallacy of the concepts that Karl Marx taught. These independent Americans can determine if Marxism is being promoted in America, and if so, is this the direction they want for America. In speaking with different people while doing my research, these people always stressed that I what I write should be just the facts.

This is not a detailed historical document, nor is it a philosophical or economic document. It is written simply, with only necessary historical documentation to give the reader a simple background so they can better understand Karl Marx and his concepts. With this understanding, they can make their own determination on how this applies to us, our children, and our grandchildren.

If this straight forward work promotes knowledgeable discussions between Americans, it will be successful. If it encourages some Americans to become even more informed by doing some independent research for their own satisfaction, it will be very successful. It is important we give thought and consideration to the America we will leave our children and grandchildren, and not just let it happen.

CONTENTS

CHAPTER 1

IS AMERICA CHANGING?

Chapter 1

On October 23rd of 2008, Barbara West, an anchor for an Orlando Florida television station conducted an interview with Senator Biden, who was at the time the nominee for Vice President on the Democratic ticket. This interview was not given mainstream media attention, even though it may have been the most important single interview of the campaign.

The interview follows:

- *WEST: You may recognize this famous quote: "From each according to his abilities to each according to his needs." That's from Karl Marx. How is Senator Obama not being a Marxist if he intends to spread the wealth around?*

  BIDEN: Are you joking? Is this a joke?

  WEST: No.

  BIDEN: Or is that a real question?

  WEST: That's a question.

  BIDEN: He is not spreading the wealth around. He's talking about giving the middle class an opportunity to get back the tax breaks they used to have.

WEST: What do you say to the people who are concerned that Barack Obama will want to turn America into a Socialist country much like Sweden?

BIDEN: I don't know anybody who thinks that, except the far right-wing of the Republican Party.

After the interview, the Obama campaign complained to the station and Senator Biden said this:

BIDEN: I was on a television station the other day and doing a satellite feed to a major network in Florida, and the anchor quotes Karl Marx, and says in a sense isn't Barack Obama Karl Marx? You know, I mean, folks, this stuff you're hearing, this stuff you're hearing on this campaign, some of it's pretty ugly, and some of the innuendo is pretty ugly.

It is even more important today that the questions by Ms. West be examined closely and also that Biden's responses to her and his comment after the interview be examined now that Obama has a history. To analyze both is important, as well as looking at the life and teachings of Karl

Marx which we will do in subsequent chapters.

The question asked in this interview was not if Barack Obama is Karl Marx. The question asked was if Barack Obama has the same beliefs that Karl Marx professed. Not only did Biden wish to downplay the question and avoid an answer, but Barack Obama has avoided answering this question as well. Obama and his friends have consistently stated that he is a friend of business. He has also stated that he wishes to cut government spending. His problem is that his actions have proven differently, and many of his statements have shown his true beliefs. Examples of this would be his off-the-cuff comments like he made to Joe the Plumber that his plan is to redistribute the wealth and his comments about him leading our country through a Fundamental Transformation. Obama also says he is for business, and then his actions are against business or he has said he wants to cut the deficit and debt but everything he does raises the debt. These are reasons the concerns Ms. West raised are valid concerns.

Do these beliefs make Obama a Marxist, Communist or Socialist? Are these the same or are they different? These terms are used to mean many different things today. I recently heard a well known television analyst say that George Soros could not be a Marxist because he has made all his money using the capitalistic system. I wanted to ask him if he thought Engels was a Marxist. After all, Engels was raised in a capitalistic home and worked for his capitalistic father in his father's privately owned business for many years. He later became an owner of his own textile mill. The money he gave to Marx to help Marx support his family and promote Marxism came directly from the proceeds of his textile mill. Marx knew where Engels was getting the money, but never refused it. Were Engels and Marx beliefs those of a Capitalist or a Marxist? Is it possible George Soros could really have Marxist beliefs even though he made his money through capitalism? It is misunderstandings and miss-statements like these that add to the confusion.

So, what did Marx mean when he made his oft-quoted statement, "From each according to his ability, to each according to his needs?" He did not make this statement in "The Communist Manifesto" but he made it in the "Critique of the Gotha

Program." Marx and Engels had a close association with the German Social Democratic movement in Germany. This was in 1875, about three decades after "The Communist Manifesto" was written. The group with whom Marx was associated, was thinking of joining another group that was led by Ferdinand Lassalle. Marx disagreed with Lassalle's ideas, and this was the reason he wrote this critique. His oft-quoted phrase was the conclusion of his description of how society would operate in the highest phase of his communistic world. It really has nothing to do with sharing wealth between the capitalist and worker because the state of his professed classless society would have been reached. An example of this final state of Marxism does not exist today nor has it ever been reached in recorded history.

Biden's answers and later comments to and about the interview with Ms. West would indicate one of two scenarios, or more likely, a combination of the two. The first scenario would be that Biden only understood the thrust of the question on a superficial level. In other words, Biden does not really know nor understands what Marx taught. It is likely that this was much of the reason for his defensive posture. The connotation of Marxism in the United States today seems to be what he stated in his comment about this being "pretty ugly." Because of this, it is more believable that Biden thought the question meant is Obama similar to Lenin, Stalin, or Mao. Marx would not have recognized their governments as Marxist and would not have identified with any of these leaders. This second scenario is why the combination of the two thoughts is the most likely scenario. Most people would think similarly. This is unfortunate. People should know the difference. The debate Marx identified had been waged prior to his birth and continues after his death. At the very least, a well known national television commentator and a candidate for Vice Presidency of the United States should understand these different concepts. The goal of this book is to help people better understand what Marx taught. If Obama is a Marxist, or if Marxism is good or bad, will then be for you to decide.

Why would Biden say this type of question is ugly? History does not show that Marx was a monster or that he killed people or imprisoned people. This is not true, however, of many of the people who have called themselves Marxists, such as Lenin, Stalin or Mao. My discussion in this book is not to insinuate in any way that the advocates of Marx's philosophies in the United States do or would follow the ruthlessness of Lenin, Stalin or Mao. I would not want anybody to believe that I believe Obama and his followers, are monsters. My observations would indicate they are good family people. Up to this point at least, I do not know of them advocating killing or jailing opponents.

However, many, maybe most Marxist advocates are not even aware they are really advocating the principles of Marx. Biden should have been honest with Ms. West and explained why he believed Obama told Joe the Plumber that his goal was to redistribute the wealth. Or what Obama meant when he stated that we were about to witness in this country a Fundamental Transformation. Biden should have explained why he and Obama had pursued this course of action over their public lives and why he believed this philosophy was correct. Instead he demeaned, dismissed, and avoided what is a basic disagreement man has had since the beginning of time.

The United States is no exception. President Woodrow Wilson was a strong advocate of many of these same principles. It was during his administration that the United States implemented one of the main means of wealth redistribution advocated by Marx in "The Communist Manifesto," the graduated income tax. President Franklin Roosevelt used the crisis of the depression to institute many other fundamental requirements advocated by Marx to achieve his goal. Obama has stated he wants to continue and advance this fundamental transformation. In 1872, Marx suggested the elements necessary for a fundamental transformation were already prevalent in the United States. These elements are even more advanced today. This will be discussed in more detail.

What is imperative is that the debate within the United States be advanced to discuss honestly the success and failure of Communism as defined by Karl Marx. Is this really the course the United States wishes to continue? In order to make an informed decision, the United States citizens need to understand what Marxism is. We need to understand who Marx was. We must look at the period of time in which he lived and how that affected his teachings. We will want to look at the history of the age old differences he discussed in detail between the oppressors and the oppressed and how that relates to us today. We must understand what Marx envisioned. We must know what he taught and why it had to be implemented so his ideal could be reached.

Once we have a basic understanding of the fundamental teachings of Marx, we can take an honest look at how, if at all, his teachings are being professed in the United States today and if we as citizens, believe they would be good for our country. When we know the different arguments, we will have a basis to ask ourselves if these policies are advancing the nation toward the Far Left, Progressive, Socialist, Communist, or Marxist utopia, and if so, is this the direction we as a nation desire.

When the question is asked if somebody who follows the teachings of a philosopher, is a disciple of that philosopher, we can discuss the question honestly even if the philosopher is Karl Marx and the alleged disciple is Barack Obama. The questioner should not be demeaned, dismissed, and even fired (as Ms. West was) because they did not practice political correctness. I believe the question was asked honestly and deserved an honest answer. It was not an ugly question. Again, Biden either did not understand the question, was afraid to answer it honestly, or it was a combination of these.

When I ask people what is their definition of a liberal or a progressive, the answers are varied. Some answers are given in the generic meaning. That is, the answer might be that a liberal or a progressive is a person who thinks ahead or has ideas that are advanced thinking. If they answer from a political perspective, the answer is politically correct depending on the political leaning of the person giving the answer. The progressive or liberal will say that it means they are compassionate and wanting to help people. The right leaning individual will say that the progressive/liberal is financially irresponsible and promotes programs that encourage people to be dependent on the government. Progressive and liberal has been interchanged in the United States for perhaps the last 150 years. The proper term to be used by the proponents will depend on the political climate at the time. Today, progressive seems to be in vogue.

Socialist is also used to mean many different things. If a person disagrees with a liberal or progressive, it is common to call him a Socialist, because it has a derogatory implication. The general implication is that the accused does not believe in capitalism and does not believe in profit or individualism. To be called a Communist or a Marxist is even worse, because now the implication is that you are bad. Not only don't you believe profits are bad, but you are willing to kill and imprison people to achieve your goals. The common belief is that Communism, Socialism and Marxism are all identical. This is not true. Marx denounced Socialism in his day, would not have recognized or agreed with twentieth century communism and denounced factions of Marxists in the 1870's and 1880's.

I believe, if Karl Marx had been born in the United States in the mid twentieth century, and had the same basic belief structure he had in the mid- to late-nineteenth century in Western Europe and England, it is entirely possible that he could have been elected to the US House of Representatives. The districts in which he would have had to run to be elected would be limited. Some possibilities would be the San Francisco Bay area, limited districts in West Los Angeles, and some Northeast districts including

Vermont, Eastern Massachusetts and possibly New York City. He would also have to have a campaign manager like Friedrich Engels to help him financially, help him manage his time and in many ways be a mother to him. As you get to know Marx as an individual and understand his philosophy better, you can decide for yourself if you agree and if many of the Progressives of today including Obama would have been comfortable with him.

CHAPTER 2

WHOSE IDEAS ARE THESE?

Karl Marx was born on May 5th in the year 1818.
His parents were Jewish, and both sides of his
family had a long history of the sons in the family
becoming rabbis. Marx's birthplace was Trier, the
oldest city in the Rhineland, which was a part of
Prussia. During the area's annexation by France, in
the time of the Napoleonic Wars, the citizens had
been exposed to new ideas such as freedom of the
press, constitutional liberty, and religious
toleration. The Rhineland was re-incorporated into
Imperial Prussia three years prior to the birth of
Marx, but hints of these liberties still lingered.
After Prussia regained control of Trier, the Jewish
People of Trier were subjected to a Prussian edict
issued in 1812, which banned them from holding
office or practicing their professions. Marx's father
changed his name and became a loyal German and
a Lutheran. Because of this change, he was able to
continue to practice law and from all outward
appearances was quite successful. He also
continued to associate with like-minded people
who had embraced the French enlightenment of
the time prior to the area, again, becoming a part
of Prussia. Among these associates was Baron
Ludwig von Westphalen, a senior official of the
Royal Prussian Provincial Government who would
later become the father-in-law of his son, Karl.

Not a great deal is known about Marx's childhood. We do know that he was not physically strong and was excused from Prussian military service because of his weak chest. We also know his early professors were liberal humanists, and that Marx was a friend of the son of Baron Ludwig von Wesphalen. The Baron also had an intelligent and attractive daughter, Jenny. She later became the wife of Karl Marx. The Baron noticed the precocious Marx boy early and took a liking to him. They were known to take long walks together. It was during these walks Marx learned to recite long passages from both Homer and Shakespeare. These passages would become a part of his writings in later years.

When it was time for young Marx to begin his college studies, he enrolled at Bonn University to study law and follow in his father's footsteps. After one year at Bonn, Marx transferred to the University of Berlin, where he continued his study of law along with history, philosophy, English, and Italian. His father was financially supporting him while he was supposedly attending lectures. Marx's real interest was philosophy. He became involved with a group that met during the evenings called the Doctors' Club. These evenings, which turned into late nights, were filled with loud conversation and quite a bit of drinking. These gatherings could have been held near most any University in the United States, Europe, or elsewhere. What was unique and important about this group, is that this was a group of Young Hegelians, and had as their main topic of discussion, the teachings of the German Philosopher, G W F Hegel.

We know this, in part, because of a letter Marx wrote to his father on November 10, 1837. This letter talked about his two great interests at that time, and it was certainly not law. One was the philosophy of Hegel, and the other was Jenny von Weshphalen, even though she was four years his senior. He later married Jenny and stayed with her until her death, but found later on, he had some differences with Hegel. Nevertheless, these early Hegelian impressions would always have an effect on his thinking.

 Hegel is credited with developing the philosophical system often called Absolute Idealism. A simplistic explanation of this system would be that everything is a process, and as this process takes place, a higher development is reached in each new stage. What is important is not what something is, but rather what it was, what it is, and what it will become. In our study of the Marx philosophy, we will see how this teaching affected his thinking and his teachings.

Marx's father died in May of 1838. By this time, young Marx had estranged himself from his family, very seldom going back to Trier. He had also stopped any pretenses of studying law and spent his time reading and discussing philosophy. His mother elected not to continue to financially support him after his father's death, and Karl Marx began his new financial life which would continue to his death. It was a life of financially living in debt and relying on help from associates and receiving aid from others.

Between 1839 and 1841, Marx wrote his doctoral dissertation "The Difference between the Democritean and Epicurean Philosophies of Nature." Even though Marx had attended both the University of Bonn and the University of Berlin, he chose to submit his dissertation to the University of Jena. This University had a reputation for awarding degrees without delay or debate. Nine days after submitting his dissertation to the University of Jena, on April 15th 1841, he was granted a Ph. D., and now was Dr. Karl Marx. Rather than beginning to teach at a University or work in any capacity, he floated between Bonn, Trier, and Cologne.

Finally, in 1842, Marx began his somewhat limited career as a Newspaper Editor in Cologne for a liberal anti-establishment newspaper. An early article he wrote was a polemic against the latest censorship instructions issued by the Prussian King. Within a few months the newspaper had been closed. This was the beginning of a life pattern for Marx. A very important event did happen during this time, however. A young man, Friedrich Engels, stopped by the newspaper office in Cologne, and Karl Marx met Friedrich Engels for the first time. Ironically, Engels was on his way to England to work in his father's cotton mill called Ermen and Engels, so he could learn the business.

In early 1843, Marx accepted a new position with another newspaper in Paris. Prior to moving to Paris, he married the patient Jenny, and after a long honeymoon financed by Jenny's mother, the newlyweds moved to Paris in November of 1843. Between this time and 1849, Marx and Jenny moved several times because of newspapers being closed, due to the writings of Marx. He was accused by the Prussian government of high crimes and misdemeanors and ordered arrested if he ever again entered Prussia. Marx was also censored because of pressure applied by the Russian Czar, after he had written about the conditions, as he saw them, in Russia. Finally in 1849, the Karl Marx family was forced to move to England, because he was not welcomed in any country of Continental Europe.

By this time, Marx and Engels had co-authored many different articles. The most famous, or infamous, depending on a person's point of view, was the "Communist Manifesto." A group, to which both Marx and Engels belonged, asked them to draft a manifesto for them. The group was comprised of German radical workers living in

Paris, who called their secret organization "Communist League." Both men prepared first drafts on their own. Engels used a question and answer format while Marx's draft was more in the form the manifesto actually took. Both men are credited with authoring the document, and both men certainly had a great influence on its final form. We will discuss the contents of this document at a later time.

During this time period, from 1843 to 1849, Marx was banished from Paris by order of the French Government. He was pressured into renouncing his Prussian citizenship and forced from Brussels. England was very tolerant of radical thinkers, and Engels owned a part of Ermen and Engels of Manchester, England. He also worked for the company and lived in Manchester. During this time, Marx became very well known among the liberal thinkers of that day. He also became acquainted with many of them, including Pierre-Joseph Proudhon.

Proudhon was a member of the French Parliament, referred to himself as a socialist, and also called himself an anarchist. Included in many of his assertions, was that property is theft. He believed socialist revolution could take place peacefully; he stated that anarchy is order without power, and advocated taxing Capitalists, and starting a government sponsored bank that would give interest free loans. Marx eventually had a split with Proudhon and wrote an anti-Proudhon tract "The Poverty of Philosophy." In this tract, Marx emphasized the struggle between classes and class warfare. He talks about the oppressed class needing to emancipate itself and create a new society. This new society will not have a new ruling class, but will have only one class, so it will be a classless society.

It was also during this time Marx started to study economics. We must remember Marx had his degree in philosophy and was first and foremost a philosopher. He had also studied history and considered himself a historian. A part of his economic education included the writings of Adam Smith, the author of "A Wealth of Nations." Marx gave a series of lectures, which were later combined into what is now called "Wage, Labour, and Capital." Among principles he developed in this series, was the principle that labour is a commodity. Capitalists will exploit this commodity; the worker. The Capitalist will develop methods to cause division of labour, and the more this is done, the less valuable and the more unnecessary the worker becomes. A modern example of this principle would be the automatic teller machines employed by banks. The more the banks use these machines, the fewer tellers the bank needs. Marx and his followers say that this practice of using machines, simplifies the work of the worker and makes him less necessary, thus he is paid a lower wage. In addition, as machines do more work, more workers are available, and when more workers compete for the same positions, wages are driven lower.

It was during this time Marx also started to develop his theory of surplus value. Surplus value is, for our purpose, the profit Capitalists "take" when a commodity is sold. Marx believed that this surplus portion of the worth of the commodity was really due to the worker. The worker created this value, and the Capitalist did nothing for it. He later wrote "Theories of Surplus Value," which in essence deplores the idea of profit being paid to the Capitalist, for which Marx stated the Capitalist did nothing.

Marx spent many hours in the British Museum after he became a resident of London. His unconventional way of life continued. He would often work and write late into the night and sleep during the day. He was also known to drink heavily at times. Marx was not a good provider, and he and Jenny had to continue relying on Engels for financial help. Engels also had to continue to remind Marx, that the manuscript he had promised a publisher was overdue. This hung over Marx, and is thought to have been a major reason for his many health problems, until finally, in 1867 volume one of "das Kapital" was published. Volumes two and three were promised by Marx, but were not published until after his death. Engels was the person to piece together the notes Marx had left for these volumes, and prepared them for the publisher.

Probably the steadiest work Marx ever had was during his time in London. In 1851 he became a regular contributor to the New York Dailey Tribune. Initially, he was to provide a column twice a week. This was cut back over time to once a week and then less and less. Since he was paid based on his contribution, this source of income became less and less. Marx lived owing money. It started while he was in Berlin at school and continued throughout his lifetime. He did inherit some money when his mother died, and Jenny inherited money when her mother died, but in both instances, it was spent quickly, and the old pattern of financial struggle would start again.

By all accounts, Marx was a kind and loving husband to Jenny, and was a loving father to his children. When he and Jenny first moved to Paris, they moved into a flat with a fellow worker of Marx with the intent of living in a commune. This lasted for two weeks, and Marx knew it would not work. History does not show that Marx was a philanderer, but cared deeply for Jenny. Apparently he did wander at least once when Jenny was visiting her mother in Trier with the children, and had an affair with the long time family maid, who later had a son. Marx is not known to have ever publicly acknowledged this child was his, but his daughter did affirm that Freddy was her half brother, after Marx had died.

Jenny and Karl Marx had six children, daughters Jenny, Laura, and Eleanor survived. It is known these sisters admired, worked, and spent social time with their father, even after their mother had died. They noted among their recollections many fond memories, such as was when the family would go to the park on Sunday afternoons and their father would tell stories and teach them Shakespeare, much like his father-in-law did when he was younger.

Even though; throughout his lifetime, Marx had written about, taught, and advanced the theory of a classless society with the elimination of Capitalism, he was not known to associate with working people. This seemed to be true of many of the philosophers of his time. We are familiar with this same pattern today. An exception was Engels. Engels lived with Mary Burns for many years, and later Mary's sister Lizzy joined the happy couple. The Burns sisters were workers in one of Engels factories, and it is believed that is how he met Mary. At the time Mary died, Engels wrote a note to Marx informing him of her death. Marx, who was never fond of Mary, did answer the note with a note of his own expressing some sympathy, but then went on to remind his friend that his funds were running low and could he send some extra.

This caused the only major rift in their relationship, but was corrected when Marx realized his mistake.

Jenny Marx died on December 2, 1881. She was unable to see her husband for the last three weeks of her life, because both were confined to hospital beds at the time. She was buried three days later and Marx was still too sick to attend her funeral. Karl Marx lived until March 14, 1883. On March 17, 1883 he was buried next to Jenny in Highgate Cemetery in London. Eleven mourners attended his funeral, including his surviving daughters, their husbands, and his long time friend Friedrich Engels.

Following is the speech given by Engels at the gravesite.

FREDERICK ENGELS SPEECH AT THE GRAVE OF KARL MARX
Highgate Cemetery, London March 17, 1883

Transcribed by Mike Lepore (mlepore@mcimail.com) in 1993.

On the 14th of March, at a quarter to three in the afternoon, the greatest living thinker ceased to think. He had been left alone for scarcely two minutes, and when we came back we found him

*in his armchair, peacefully gone to sleep -- but
for ever.*

*An immeasurable loss has been sustained both
by the militant proletariat of Europe and
America, and by historical science, in the death
of this man. The gap that has been left by the
departure of this mighty spirit will soon enough
make itself felt.*

*Just as Darwin discovered the law of
development or organic nature, so Marx
discovered the law of development of human
history: the simple fact, hitherto concealed by an
overgrowth of ideology, that mankind must first
of all eat, drink, have shelter and clothing,
before it can pursue politics, science, art,
religion, etc.; that therefore the production of the
immediate material means, and consequently the
degree
of economic development attained by a given people
or during a given epoch, form the foundation upon
which the state institutions, the legal conceptions,
art, and even the ideas on religion, of the people
concerned have been evolved, and in the light of
which they must, therefore, be explained, instead of
vice versa, as had hitherto been the case.*

*But that is not all. Marx also discovered the special
law of motion governing the present-day capitalist
mode of production, and the bourgeois society that
this mode of production has created. The discovery
of
surplus value suddenly threw light on the problem,
in trying to solve which all previous investigations,
of*

both bourgeois economists and socialist critics, had been groping in the dark.

Two such discoveries would be enough for one lifetime. Happy the man to whom it is granted to make

even one such discovery. But in every single field which Marx investigated -- and he investigated very many fields, none of them superficially -- in every field, even in that of mathematics, he made independent discoveries.

Such was the man of science. But this was not even half the man. Science was for Marx a historically dynamic, revolutionary force. However great the joy with which he welcomed a new discovery in some

theoretical science whose practical application perhaps it was as yet quite impossible to envisage, he

experienced quite another kind of joy when the discovery involved immediate revolutionary changes in

industry, and in historical development in general. For example, he followed closely the development of

the discoveries made in the field of electricity and recently those of Marcel Deprez.

For Marx was before all else a revolutionist. His real mission in life was to contribute, in one way or another, to the overthrow of capitalist society and of the state institutions which it had brought into being, to contribute to the liberation of the modern proletariat, which he was the first to make conscious of its

own position and its needs, conscious of the conditions of its emancipation. Fighting was his element.

And he fought with a passion, a tenacity and a success such as few could rival. His work on the first

Rheinische Zeitung (1842), the Paris Vorwarts (1844), the Deutsche Brusseler Zeitung (1847), the Neue

Rheinische Zeitung (1848-49), the New York Tribune (1852-61), and, in addition to these, a host of

militant pamphlets, work in organisations in Paris, Brussels and London, and finally, crowning all, the formation of the great International Working Men's Association -- this was indeed an achievement of which its founder might well have been proud even if he had done nothing else.

And, consequently, Marx was the best hated and most calumniated man of his time. Governments, both

absolutist and republican, deported him from their territories. Bourgeois, whether conservative or ultra-democratic, vied with one another in heaping slanders upon him. All this he brushed aside as though it were a cobweb, ignoring it, answering only when extreme necessity compelled him. And he died beloved, revered and mourned by millions of revolutionary fellow workers -- from the mines of

Siberia to California, in all parts of Europe and
America -- and I make bold to say that, though he
may
have had many opponents, he had hardly one
personal enemy.
His name will endure through the ages, and so also
will his work.

Engels' burial speech
http://www.marxists.org/archive/marx/works/1883deat/burial.ht
m (1 of 2) [23/08/2000 17:50:50]

I wonder if Engels really realized how truthful his last sentence was. When Biden was questioned and went on to belittle his interviewer, did Biden have any idea who Marx really was or what he taught. Now that we have a better idea of who Marx was, we will examine some of his writings. By doing this, you can then make up your own mind as to who might or might not, knowingly or unknowingly be a follower of Marx.

CHAPTER 3

WHAT IS FAIR?

A move was being made to unite two factions of the German Social Democratic party. The party congress was to take place in the town of Gotha. The faction to which Marx and Engels belonged sent a draft of the proposed program for a unified party to them. The congress was to take place in May 1875. Offering perhaps Marx's most detailed pronouncement on programmatic matters of revolutionary strategy, the document discusses among other topics, the period of transition from Capitalism to Communism. In addition, Marx does address what he considers a fair distribution of income means in his society. The phrase "a society should be fair" is used very often in politics and especially when referring to the tax system and social programs of modern society. Although it is used often, it is very seldom, if ever defined. Marx directly addresses what Marxism considers a "fair" distribution. In his analysis he understands that a transition period is required to make the fundamental transformation from Capitalism to Communism.

Marx defines what a fair distribution of the proceeds of labor would be. He does this by first defining the proceeds of labor as the total social product. We would refer to this as our gross national product, or the value of all goods and services produced by our society. This total social product would include what Marx calls "surplus value. " In his major work "das Kapital" he roughly defines surplus value as that new value created by workers in excess of their own labor-cost, a value which Marx said was appropriated by the capitalist as gross profit, and which is the basis of capital accumulation. We must remember that in this new world of Marxism the Capitalist will no longer exist and all capital producing property, including land will be under community ownership, or owned by the "people."

For our purposes in this analysis, we will take the liberty of referring to the owner of the community property as "the people". In the fair distribution of the social product, the people must first deduct from the total social product the cost of replacing the means of production. Just as in the world of Capitalism, the machinery and other means of production will suffer from depletion and must be replaced at some time. Community ownership does not give a machine an infinite life, so depreciation is taken into consideration.

Next, the people would deduct necessary resources to expand the productive forces to meet the demand of an expanding population. Marx does not specify that included in this cost, the people would allow for research and development costs. We do not know if this was intentional. My belief is that it was intentional, because of the many times in his other writings he commented about how Capitalists would exploit the worker by developing new means of production in order to eliminate workers and/or make them less significant. The automated tellers in banks would probably be an innovation Marx would have, like Obama, dammed because it eliminates workers. This is speculation on the author's part.

Marx continues by explaining how the people must set aside part of the social product necessary to allow for insurance or provide reserves to be used in case of accidents or dislocations caused by natural calamities, etc. These deductions are all good business practices and are an economic necessity. The magnitude of funds set aside would be determined according to available means and forces, and partly by computation of probabilities, but they are in no way calculable by equity, so stated Marx. We would add that, although these are sound business practices, we do not understand how this allocation can be used without considering equity. But then in that new world, owner equity would not exist.

From the remaining social product, prior to the worker receiving his share of fair distribution, the general cost of administration must be deducted. This would not include wages of administrators, since they are workers and would be included when calculating the final portion of the fair distribution. Administration would include the cost of power, supplies, and other necessary expenses. Marx makes the claim that administration cost would be less from the very first day of transition and would be reduced as the new society developed. When attempts at Marxism have been tried in the real world, actual practice did not support his theory.

In addition, the people must allow for the cost of facilities and services intended for the common satisfaction of needs. This would include funds for schools, health services and other necessary social responsibilities. These would be the functions supported by local, state and federal taxes in our system today. The cost of a military would be greatly reduced under a Marxist society and ideally eliminated. We will understand this statement more after we have read the chapter on the "Communist Manifesto." Even when this is considered, Marx makes the statement that this cost, unlike the administrative cost, would from the outset grow considerably in comparison with current costs and grow in proportion, as the fundamentally transformed society grows. This assertion would certainly appear to be correct based on experiments. The social services necessary to provide for the common satisfaction of needs is greatly expanded under the Marxist system. After this distribution is made, the people must now make a distribution for those persons who are unable to work. The distribution amount is an amount based on the need of the person unable to work. Marx does not detail who these persons might be, but certainly it would include those disabled for any reason, perhaps the elderly, maybe single mothers, but would include those the society defined as people unable to work. Even within our current system, we see the Progressives, Liberals and Leftists expanding this definition continuously.

The transformation will change from the Capitalistic system to the Marxist system. Each worker in the early stages of the transformation would receive his certificate for his labor. This certificate is like a paycheck. It would be equal to his labor contribution less the deductions for the common causes. In many ways this would not be that much different from today, except no provision is made to investors or owners for the risk they have taken for investing their capital. The community is the owner of all capital producing assets so no allowance need be made. All people are workers and receive value for their labor only. The equality at this time is that a standard measurement is used for everybody. This means that all people might not receive the same net amount on their certificate, but the measurement used to calculate the amount would be the same. It would be similar to everybody having the same wage per product produced. If one person produces more products they would receive more on their certificate.

Marx goes on however, to explain that even this measurement is not fair and the full transformation has not yet taken place. Each worker is different. One might be physically or mentally superior to another and so supplies more labor and produces more products in the same amount of time as the inferior worker. Equal right cannot recognize these differences, because everyone is a worker. When these differences are recognized for purposes of measurement, then the rule of equality no longer exists. In addition, other differences may exist such as one worker is married, another is not; one has more children than another and so on and so forth. These differences must be considered for true fair equality. One worker is not to become richer than the other. Marx explains in his society, this would not be fair.

He further explains, "In a higher phase of communist society, after the enslaving subordination of the individual to the division of labor, and therewith also the antithesis between mental and physical labor, has vanished; after labor has become not only a means of life but life's prime want; after the productive forces have also increased with the all-round development of the individual, and all the springs of cooperative wealth flow more abundantly-only then can the narrow horizon of bourgeois right be crossed in its entirety and society inscribe on its banner: FROM EACH ACCORDING TO HIS ABILITY, TO EACH ACCORDING TO HIS NEEDS!"

It is important to remember that Marx was a Philosopher. My reading of philosophy has taught me that philosophy is the study of man as the philosopher believes man should be, or will become, and not as human nature is. Differences in man's physical ability, mental capacity, ambition level, etc. have always existed. Rewards bring out the best and worst in people. In Marx's world, the reward a worker receives for working at his top productive level, would be his satisfaction and knowledge that he is making his maximum contribution to society, and fulfilling what has become his prime want in this new world. Even within the world of the Progressive, Liberal and Leftist, I have not seen examples that this transformation in human nature has occurred or even begun. This is, however, what fairness would be in this world of Fundamental Transformation for which Marx and the Progressives, Liberals and Leftists desire and strive.

CHAPTER 4

CAUSING THE CHANGES

CHAPTER 4

All of Europe was changing economically and politically. England was leading the way with both its political reforms and the industrial revolution. France had overthrown the Bourbon Monarchy and survived Napoleon, but after different attempts at different governments was once again ruled by a Bourbon monarch, Louis Philippe. The German states were still independent with no central cohesive government. Prussia was the strongest of these independent states and ruled by Frederic Wilhelm. The feudal system, although still present on the continent; was in a state of decline as economic change was dramatically changing the European economic and social landscapes.

Liberalism was raising its head with many prolific philosophers and writers, bringing forth new thoughts that were contrary to common beliefs of the day. These thoughts were being published and discussed in England and throughout the continent, but primarily in France and Germany. Marx was well known in these liberal circles as well as by the authorities. He had already been forced to leave Germany because of his radical ideas. He had many articles published. The Tsar of Russia, even though Marx had never been in Russia, complained to the government of France concerning an article written by Marx about the conditions as he saw them in Russia; consequently Marx was expelled from France. Among other issues, these writings of Marx and others exposed many workers issues including low wages, long working hours, poor working conditions, and poor living conditions.

Another major issue of the day was the franchise, or who had the right to vote. There were two different schools of thought that wanted the current number of people who were allowed to vote to be expanded. The first school simply wanted the franchise to be widened so that the lower bourgeoisie could vote. The second thought was much more expansive. This thought was universal suffrage, or every man having the right to vote. The problem was that the monarchy was totally opposed to any electoral reform, and refused to allow any changes. As a result, the reformers joined together and held reform banquets where they could voice their thoughts and opinions and listen to others. The forced cancellation of one of these banquets was the catalyst for the start of these revolutions, now known as the Revolutions of 1848.

In addition to the above unsettling times, bad harvests were happening all over Europe. These bad harvests had their own negative effects causing high food prices and long food lines. With the low wages being paid and rapidly increasing food costs, it was a difficult time for the peasant and the worker. None of the governments did anything to assist the worker in these difficult economic times.

Within the different independent German kingdoms, including Prussia which was the strongest, a distrust of France was ever present, especially after Napoleon had so easily dominated these different German states. A German nationalist spirit was consequently growing and was most vocal with students and with people who had lived through the Napoleonic times.

The revolutions of 1848 began in France in February of that year. Louis Philippe was forced to ask for the resignation of his Prime Minister and when this resignation did not satisfy the revolutionists, he abdicated his throne. Louis Philippe's intent was to abdicate his throne in favor of his grandson; however, his grandson was never crowned. Instead, a Second Republic was established with elected officials to run the government, thus ending the reign of the Bourbons for a second time. The new government proved to be more restrictive than the people anticipated and a failed insurrection took place in June of 1848. In December of the same year, another election was held and the winner of that election was Louis Napoleon. He was elected with the overwhelming support of the peasant population. Within a few short years he suspended the elected assembly and established the Second French Empire. History did appear to repeat itself.

All was not lost in the revolution however. Workdays had been shortened, the right to vote was extended to all males, freedom of speech, assembly, and association were proclaimed. Some political prisoners were released. Also, a system of "National Workshops" was instituted that was suppose to guarantee a job to every citizen. The revolution in France also spread throughout Europe. For instance, in Austria the Diet (parliament) demanded the resignation of Prince Metternich, the conservative State Chancellor and Foreign Minister. The Hapsburgs, the long standing ruling family of Austria, did, however, retain power despite some uprisings throughout the Empire.

The Revolution also spread to the German States with unification of these states being a major objective of the revolutionists. A National Assembly was convened in May of 1848. The main objectives of the founders of this National Assembly were to write a national constitution for the German States, create a central German government, and to guarantee freedom of the press, trial by jury, and other basic rights to all German citizens.

Even though the Assembly was not truly a unified body, they did manage to unify enough to offer Kaiser Frederick Wilhelm IV of Prussia the unifying crown of all German states. He refused that crown and stated that man did not have the authority to grant the crown, but that authority rested only with God. The Assembly was subsequently disbanded by military force and, in essence, the Revolution of 1848 was over.

Friedrich Engels was an active participant in the revolution. Karl Marx certainly contributed to the mood in Europe that contributed to the revolution, but was not an active participant. After the revolution, in 1850, Marx and Engels wrote the "Address of the Central Committee to the Communist League." In this address, they presented a political strategy to use in the event of another revolution. Engels later wrote in 1885, that this same strategy was still appropriate for the next upheaval.

According to this address, the revolution of 1848 was not just a revolution of the proletariat, but also a revolution of what Marx called the petty-bourgeois democrats. This would be the class of people positioned between the nobility and feudal lords still existing in Germany, and the worker or proletariat. Marx acknowledged that some of the goals of both groups; that is, the proletariat and petty bourgeoisie, were similar, but not totally identical. The change the petty bourgeoisie wanted in social conditions, for instance, is that life will be made comfortable and tolerable for them without thought of the worker. The petty bourgeoisie wanted the government to be curtailed and supported by taxes on big landowners and nobility. They also looked for state sponsored loans on which lower interest rates would apply. In addition, a complete abolition of feudalism would be completed which would allow for direct control or ownership of property to be more widespread. These goals, according to Marx, were not the goals of the proletariat.

The proletariat, according to Marx, did not want the revolution to end, but to be permanent until all classes possessing private property have been forced out of their positions and the proletariat has conquered state power. He states further that for the proletariat, the issue cannot be the alteration of private property but only its annihilation, not the smoothing over of class antagonisms, but the abolition of classes, not the improvement of existing society but the foundation of a new one.

How did Marx say these goals should be accomplished? After all, the Revolution of 1848 did not bring about the changes he had envisioned. We must keep in mind the time and conditions in which these events occurred. In Germany, as in Poland, Russia and other parts of Europe, feudalism still existed. It had been abolished in certain parts of Europe and it was evident that it would be abolished throughout all of Europe. Marx stated that when this happened, as it had elsewhere, the petty bourgeoisie would want the land to go to the peasant as free property or property owned by the peasant. According to Marx, this was wrong and the property should become common property or property of the state and shared by all in the community. He also foresaw the petty bourgeoisie striving for a government that is decentralized with the utmost possible autonomy and independence for the communities and provinces. This, according to Marx, should not be the goal of the worker, but the workers must instead strive for a single and centralized government with the centralization of power held in the hands of the state authority.

Marx further stated that there were several things workers must be doing to accomplish these goals. They must constantly be disrupting the regular course of social order. This would include, but not be limited to, them trying their utmost to have all productive forces, all means of transport such as railways and all factories concentrated in the hands of the state and controlled by the state. Methods by which this can be done would be, for instance, supporting confiscation of private capital producing property by the state, demanding progressive taxes with tax rates so high that capital will be ruined.

He further states that when regulation or curtailment of national debt is attempted, the workers must demand that the national debt not be controlled. Instead, Marx says, the worker shall cause the government to become bankrupt. This will help bring about the Fundamental Transformation called for by Marx.

CHAPTER 5

THE RESULTS

In order to better understand what Marx believed and taught, we will look at some of his different writings. One of these is "The German Ideology." He wrote this with Engels in 1845 and 1846. At this time England was becoming a manufacturing giant and trading around the globe. This was also the earlier years of the Victorian age in England. France was under the liberal monarchy of Louis Philippe and Prussia was ruled by autocrat Friedrich Wilhelm IV. Europe was also in the midst of an economic downturn, which resulted in a revolution in 1848. Marx and Engels were involved in the philosophical arguments that were prevalent within their circles. One of the purposes of writing "The German Ideology" was to support a materialistic approach to philosophy as opposed to the more common idealistic approach of Hegel and other philosophers. In order to show the differences of these approaches, Marx states that it is necessary to go back through history and look at man in reality.

He does this by showing how the division of labor developed throughout different stages in history and how ownership of property evolved eventually to become private property. It is necessary to show his reasoning in these areas so we can understand Marx's definition of communism. His premise is that a man's worth coincides with what he produces and how he earns his means for subsistence. This is essential because it determines how man interacts with other men, which determines interaction between tribes, families, and eventually nations. This interaction was critical in determining how common property ownership developed into private property ownership.

In the beginning of recorded history, each man was responsible for taking care of himself and his family. Man would have to hunt, fish, and gather only for himself and his family. No premise of any sort of land or capital ownership was present. The only activity that resembled a division of labor would be activity within a family setting; men, women and children all had different responsibilities within the family structure. The first form of ownership of any type of property was ownership by tribes or tribal ownership. The formation of tribes started when two or more families would join together and live in a rudimentary society. The forms of production for subsistence were similar to what the families did, that being hunting and fishing, and agriculture or gathering which would take place over a large geographical area. Society became more developed as numbers of people in the tribes increased. Tribes became more organized with the advent of tribal chieftains and eventually the formation of councils.

The second form of ownership which developed is very important for purposes of our discussion. Marx calls this the "ancient communal and State ownership" phase. This was the joining together of many different tribes into a city. The joining together might have come about because of an agreement between tribes or the conquest of one tribe by another. This phase brought about the concept of slavery. The conquering tribe began to make the conquered tribe its slaves. These slaves became the property of the conquering tribe under tribal law. Thus began the ownership of property. The property was both moveable and immovable. The ownership was communal, even the ownership of moveable property or slaves. We also see division of labor becoming more defined, caused by many reasons including antagonisms arising between different societies or cities or states. No longer did a classless society exist, but instead a two tiered class society was developing that consisted of citizens as one class, and slaves as the other.

During this time of war and conquest, which included the time of the rise and fall of Rome, different classes of privilege and wealth continued to develop. With this development, mobility between classes became more and more difficult until it was almost impossible to move from one to the other. Ownership of property by individuals and concentration of this ownership began early in Rome. Laws like the Licinian Agrarian Law came into existence. The intent of this law was to spread ownership to more individuals.   Despite the intent of the law, the concentration of ownership continued even as more land was captured by the Empire and at the time of capture it was held as public land.

After the fall of the Roman Empire, the third form of ownership developed. This was feudal or estate property. Much of civilized society changed. These changes came about, partly because of the changes in the method and extent of trade and what was the beginning of a rudimentary form of manufacturing. The early stages of the feudal society were predominantly a rural society as opposed to urban. Marx likens ownership of property at this time to be similar to the tribal and community ownership that existed prior to the Roman Empire era. The classes of society were now the citizen or nobility and the serf or slave. With the growth of the cities, due partly because serfs were escaping and going to the city, a new form of property started to develop.   This new form of property was cooperative property or property consisting chiefly in the labor of people. This was developing through the feudal organization of trades.

In the rural areas, there was landed property with the nobility as the capitalist and the serf as the laborer. In the city, with the development of guilds, this new type of ownership was forming. It consisted of the master who had journeymen and apprentices as his workers. Division of labor was becoming more and more defined. Private property was being accumulated by landowners, as well as these masters or businessmen. In addition to the master producer, another form of owner or capitalist was developing, and that was the merchant.

As the division of labor became more and more defined, the worker lost more and more freedom, according to Marx and Engels. Now each man would have a particular sphere of activity that was exclusive. In other words, the worker would have a specific job or function in the production of a product. This was unlike the early man who could be a fisherman one day, a hunter the next, a gatherer the next day, or he could do all three in the same day if he so chose. Now the worker would perform the same function each and every day. Man, since he has lost control, is now enslaved due to the division of labor the same way the serf would be enslaved in Marx's reasoning.

This enslavement, said Marx, developed because of the different factors that caused these events to take place. After all, history is the account of how man develops to satisfy his needs and wants. The early accounts are of man satisfying his needs of food, shelter and clothing. After he was able to fulfill these primary needs, he found he had other needs and also wants as well. This is the productive side of history. The social side of history began with man relating to other members of his family, then a tribe, then cities, states and nations. What came about because of these happenings, were contradictions between the interest of the individual person and the interest of the community as a whole.

Private property and division of labor not only brought about the development of the state, but also formed two basic classes in society. Marx and Engels refer to these classes as the proletariat and the bourgeoisie, or what we will refer to as the worker and the capitalist. Marx further put forth the idea that any political struggle is a struggle between the classes. This would include struggles for the type and form of government. For instance, will the government be democratic or autocratic. All these struggles, according to Marx, are struggles between the rich and poor or between the capitalist and worker. Class warfare is always the issue. When a class is struggling for dominance, such as the worker struggling for dominance within a political structure, a fundamental transformation of that political and economic format must occur. This fundamental transformation must be such that the worker class conquers political power, so that its interest is represented as the general interest. This is the goal of the communist, according to Marx.

The goal and ultimate result of this fundamental transformation is a classless society. At that time, each person would be equal and consequently individuals would not have as their primary goal to fulfill their individual wants, but instead would have as their only goal to contribute entirely to and for the betterment of the community. No productive private property would exist. It must be clarified that productive private property means property that produces capital, such as factories, productive land, ect. This type of property would be owned by the state or the community. Disparities in incomes would be eliminated, other than those disparities based on need. All would receive equally regardless of individual capabilities, ambition or work ethic. There would be only one class of people in all regards, so class warfare would not be needed and not practiced. All are equal and free according to Marx.

CHAPTER 6

NECESSARY ACTIONS

This document is perhaps better known as "The Communist Manifesto." It came about because of a group of radical German workers who were living in Paris formed a secret association called the "League of the Just." They later renamed this secret association "Communist League." In 1847 this group commissioned two of the newer members of the group, Karl Marx and Friedrich Engels, to draft a manifesto for their association. Marx and Engels begin the project, independent of the other. Engels had used a question- and-answer approach in his draft, and Marx used the approach that was adopted for the final draft. Although Marx is most closely associated with the final product, Engels also deserves much credit for his contribution. As in many of the writings by Marx, Engels did final editing and drafting.

It has been claimed that this document is the most widely read and most influential single document of modern socialism. The manifesto has been translated into virtually every language including English, German, Russian, and French. The original was written in 1847, and translated into French just before the revolution of 1848. Even though the manifesto has been widely read and studied in the world of socialism, it has not been widely read, taught, or understood in the United States, and probably most of the modern Western democracies. In spite of not being taught, studied, or understood in the United States, it is alarming how many of the principles and guidelines contained within the manifesto are practiced and followed by Progressives, Liberals and Leftists. Even though many people think of the manifesto as being an economic document, it is a philosophical document, using many of the principles taught by Hegel. This should not be a surprise to anyone, since Marx held a PhD in Philosophy and both Marx and Engels were students of Hegelism in their early years.

"A spectre is haunting Europe-the spectre of Communism." This is the opening statement of the Manifesto. In the beginning of the first section the opening line is "The history of all hitherto existing society is the history of class struggles." We have seen this theme continually in Marx's writing. The opening paragraphs of the Manifesto explain the history of the development of society similar to his historical development in the German Ideology. Throughout this development Marx shows his ideas of how one class of society was oppressed by another group of society. He refers to these groups as the Oppressors and the Oppressed. The Oppressors are the class that was the economically blessed and the Oppressed are the class who are economically depressed, according to this theory. In modern society the correlating terms might be the millionaires and billionaires oppressing the rest of society, or the one percent oppressing the ninety-nine percent. Marx calls these classes the Bourgeoisie, who were the oppressors and the Proletariat who were the oppressed.

As the Manifesto emphasizes, the bourgeoisie were the root of all problems of their day, just as the one percent would be presumed to be the root of all problems, today. The nexus between man and man, then and now, is no longer some feudal tie of a serf being bound to a "natural superior," but is only the self interest and monetary accumulating desires of the superior. In addition, the oppressing group reduces all relationships, including family and religion to selfish capital accumulation activities. In his quest for self satisfaction, the Capitalist (bourgeoisie) must continue to change modes of production because these new innovations will increase his return at the expense of the worker. These new innovations also reduce the worth of workers as divisions of labor become more and more developed. The worth of the worker also decreases as machines do more and more of the work, and fewer and fewer workers are needed to produce the same product. Consequently, the Capitalist must exploit new and other frontiers to discover more markets for its products.

The net result to society, according to Marx is the exploitation of these newly discovered markets, more misuse of resources and more destruction of land to recover these resources for use by the evil Capitalist. The Capitalists mismanagement of the production cycle also cause periods of overproduction that result in drastic downturns within these economic cycles and thus cause despair for the worker. The worker is reduced to being a pawn of the cycle and his life support is at the whim of the Capitalist since the worker is a paycheck to paycheck participant.

The proletariat develops from different sectors of the workplace. The person who was and still is a worker is perhaps the majority of this class. Also included are the artisans who were striving to be shop owners or capitalist craftsmen of some sort, but were driven into the worker class because of the bourgeoisies. This came about because the small shop owner could not compete with the larger shop owners and had to go out of business. The craftsman could no longer compete because of some new method of production that renders his skills worthless. The reaction of these changes within the proletariat is described by Marx. He explains how unions or groups of workers will be formed. These groups will destroy the wares and means of production that compete with them for labor; they will burn factories, will revert to other means of force and also cause riots. In modern

Western democracies this is commonly referred to as protests and revered and encouraged by, Progressives, Leftist, and Liberals.

Prior to open revolution, the difference between the bourgeoisies and proletariat will become more and more pronounced. The modern proletariat will sink deeper and deeper into poverty, instead of rising as industry progresses, according to Marx. A wider and wider gap between classes will ensue. This difference will show that the bourgeoisie is unfit any longer to be the ruling class in society. The advances in industry and technological developments will be the reason for their downfall. What Marx did not predict was how the proletariat would benefit from these advances and how their standard of living would improve. If Marx were writing today, one could only speculate that he would, in all likelihood say the gap between the capitalist and worker was oppressing the worker and this gap was unfair. It is because of this, Marx predicts the fall of the bourgeoisie and the rise of the proletariat, which would mean eventually only one class would exist. The necessity for class warfare would no longer exist.

Marx explains the goals of the Communist party. He states that these goals not only should be, but are, the goals of the entire proletariat. His position is that the communists' best understand these goals, which are first the overthrow of the bourgeois supremacy and conquest of political power by the proletariat. He explains that this is not a new or invented position. The assertion is that this struggle has been waged throughout history. The struggle did not end with the revolutions of 1848. It did not end with the death of Marx or Engels. It did not end with the turn of any century or with the conclusion of any war. The struggle is not contained within any specific national border nor confined to one form of government. The struggle has existed from recorded history and will continue beyond our time. Indeed, this struggle has broken into a ferocious war within the borders of the United States.

The theory or goal of the Communists, after gaining political power is obtained, would be the abolition of capital producing private property. We are fortunate that Marx does explain what this means and entails. First, Marx emphasizes that the change in how property is owned or controlled is not unique to the Communist movement. Throughout history these relationships have changed and evolved. The modern relationship of how private property is held is the final and most complete expression of the system of producing and appropriating products, which is based on class antagonisms and on the exploitation of the many by the few, he states. Private property for this purpose does not mean the property of the petty artisan and of the small peasant. This was a form and type of property ownership that preceded the bourgeois form. This is a common misconception of Marxism, that is, that Marxism advocates eliminating private ownership of all private property, as stated by so many pundits today. This is not accurate according to the Manifesto. The Socialists of this time period did advocate and practice sharing of all forms of property including personal property. This is one of the main distinctions between Socialism and Marxism and why Marx is known to have stated that he is not a Socialist. Of course, later in his life, he also said he was not a Marxist either, based on what people had professed under his name.

So, then, what private property is to be abolished as private property and become property of the state or property owned in common? This would be any property that uses wage labor to increase its capital. It would be productive property of any type. Certainly factories and rental properties, farm land or land for other types of production, businesses of all types and any other property deemed by the state to be property that exploits wage –labor. This definition is meant to be all encompassing. Marx recognizes that this change will not be done in one transaction. This transition will be a gradual process. The proletariat will have to use its political supremacy to produce means by which the transformation can be made complete.

Marx outlines what these measures should be. He recognizes that the specifics may vary depending on the country, the peculiarities of that country and how advanced it might be. We will explore the measures he details that are peculiar to the United States today and then look at what is happening in the political arena in the United States.

The first measure that Marx outlines is to abolish all private ownership land and apply all rents of this land to public purposes. At first glance, most would say that this has not, nor is it happening in the United States. It is true that the government, neither State nor Federal has taken the Empire State building, Chrysler building or Trump Tower and put the rents directly into its treasury. It is also safe to say, I believe, that if this was proposed, a huge uproar would be heard throughout the nation. However, States have started to use the principle of eminent domain to advance this measure. When a government is able to claim private property through the doctrine of eminent domain so the community can have another private person to develop and own the property, because the government would then receive higher taxes on said property, it seems that this measure is starting to be employed. It becomes entrenched when the courts uphold the principle, which has taken place. Does this mean we are now at the top of the slippery slope and starting to slide quickly?

The second measure Marx outlines is a heavy progressive or graduated income tax. A graduated income tax was first introduced in the United States during the Civil War and lasted until 1872. It was again introduced in 1894 and then declared unconstitutional. Then in 1913, the 16th Amendment to the Constitution made the income tax a part of the Constitution. The first rates were graduated but probably could not be defined as heavy. The rates ranged from one to seven percent. One percent was levied on income from $0 to $20,000. For the overwhelming number of Americans the rate was 1%. However, this was just the beginning. The Progressives under Woodrow Wilson did not take long to implement confiscatory rates as Marx called for in the Manifesto. In 1917 the new tax code had its bottom rate doubled from one percent to two percent and the top rate went to sixty-seven percent. The rest is history. The tax rates and then tax deductions that determine what taxes are paid, have been argued ever since 1913. Marx would have argued for very high rates with few if any deductions, since this was a way to transfer property from one class to another. It is a very effective way to wage the type of class warfare he knew was necessary to bring about the fundamental transformation of society he advocated.

In addition to a heavy progressive graduated income tax, Marx said that the right of inheritance should also be abolished. The heirs of the deceased would receive nothing and the state would receive 100% of the deceased's property. If an individual owned a factory, at his death the state would now possess this productive property. The Progressives under Wilson introduced the modern estate tax in 1916. The high rate at that time was ten percent. The top rate has been as high as seventy-seven percent, but has never risen to one hundred percent advocated by Marx, yet. However, I did hear the Chairman of the Democratic Party, Debbie Wasserman Schultz, say the other day, that a one hundred percent estate tax would be just and right.

Marx states that the centralization of credit in the hands of the State, by means of a national bank capitalized with common or state capital, that maintains an exclusive monopoly, is a part of the transition process. In 1913, Woodrow Wilson signed the Federal Reserve Act into law. Once again, Progressive Wilson is at the center of adopting one of Marx's primary principals. What we have seen take place, in addition to the regulation of credit by the Federal Reserve, is an activist Congress dictating to private banks as to whom they must lend their private capital. This principle was introduced in 1933 under President Franklin Roosevelt with the adoption of the Home

Owners Home Act. The result was a record number of bad loans and foreclosures. The Marx concept was brought to a new level when Representative Frank and Senator Dodd forced private banks to lend to high risk borrowers under quasi government corporations that purchased these bad loans from the banks. Progressives have consistently tried to centralize credit and lending institutions. The latest being the "Dodd-Frank Wall Street Reform and Consumer Protection Act."

The next measurement for this transition called for the centralization of the communication and transportation industries in the hands of the State. We have seen this being done on a continuing basis through the use of regulations and legislation. Progressives, Liberals, and Leftists are constantly passing regulations to control both the communication and transportation industries. These regulations and laws, for the most part, other than Amtrak and perhaps Chrysler and General Motors, have not put ownership under the State. Nevertheless, effective control has been confiscated through the employment of regulation and legislation. The Federal Communication Commission was adopted as a part of the Communications Act of 1934 under Progressive Franklin Roosevelt. The Department of Transportation came into existence in 1966 under another Progressive, President Lyndon Johnson. Both of these regulate institutions constantly implement more control by writing more regulations.

Marx then summarizes these necessary measures by extolling these means to complete the centralization process. He explains this is how the FUNDAMENTAL TRANSFORMATION will have to be affected. Through these measures the class warfare will no longer be necessary or even possible since all people will be equal and no class will exist.

CHAPTER 7

WE STILL HAVE A CHOICE

Karl Marx was a philosopher. He and Engels set themselves apart because they dealt with not just the ideological, but also with what they called the materialist conception of their philosophical world. Engels explained this in a note he wrote in September of 1890. In that note, he stated that we must recognize that "the ultimately determining element in history is the production and reproduction of real life." Although the economic situation is the basis, all elements of society are a part of life. These other elements include the political, philosophical theories, and religious theories, as well as other elements. Marx stated, and then described, what should be the ultimate outcome of his constant class warfare and class struggle. The ultimate warfare and struggle would end when all people were equal so no class would exist. He had asserted that if only one class exists, then all are equal and no class exists. This final result of no class distinctions would be in all elements of society, including the political and economic elements. The struggle for the achievement of his goal has gone on from the beginning of recorded history and has still not been successfully achieved. Attempts have been made on smaller stages as well as larger or national stages.

Marx did describe in more detail how society would function in his classless state. To see this more closely, we must go back to his statement quoted by Ms West in her interview with Biden "EACH ACCORDING TO HIS ABILITY AND EACH ACCORDING TO HIS NEED." What does this really mean based on his definition? Marx explained in other writings that it does not mean contrary, to many assertions, that nobody would have private ownership of any property. No private ownership of property that produced capital could exist. This includes private ownership of any means that would enable a private person to profit from the labor of another person. Unlike the Socialists of the day, however, those private necessities of life would not have to be shared. These necessities of life would include living quarters, food, partners and children. It was the Socialists who needed the village to raise a child and not the Marxists. Marx did state, on many occasions, that he did not agree with the Socialists of his day, including Owen, who established Socialist societies in England and then in the United States.

Although some private ownership would exist in the world Marx envisioned, it would only be what was necessary, according to the needs of the worker and not based on his ability, ambition, or work ethic. If, for instance, professional sports teams existed in Marx's ultimate world, the star of the team would be paid according to his need, and not his ability, as would all other players on the team. If the star were not married and had no children, his need would be less, than say the last substitute who had a wife and four children. In this example, the last substitute would receive more because of his greater need. If the parking lot attendant had a wife and four children, he would receive the same as the substitute and more than the star. All workers in the same need situation, a wife and four children, for instance, would receive the same since they would have the same need. Ability, ambition, and work ethic would have no relevance on financial or value reward. Marx explains all would be fine in this world because no one would oppress anyone else. It would work, Marx explains, because in this world there is no need or desire for financial or political supremacy. Each worker would be doing the work they wanted to do. They would strife to excel and do their very best, because satisfaction in performing at the workers highest ability would be the reward each worker would seek. His contribution to the community becomes the workers goal.

Progressives, Liberals and Leftists today, would argue that they are, in fact, Capitalists and not Marxists. They want us to believe they are not striving for what Marx thought would ultimately prevail after the revolution and takeover by the proletariat to eliminate all economic and political classes. However, when we look at the progression of change within the United Sates, especially since Woodrow Wilson, this is not borne out by the facts. The advance toward the Marxist society has not been a straight line. Bumps in that road have occurred. Barry Goldwater certainly brought attention to what was happening, and President Ronald Reagan was actually able to arrest the movement, momentarily. But, for the most part, the advance has continued. Perhaps the most glaring example is the change in definitions. What used to be considered mainstream is now considered to be right-wing radicalism. Two of these glaring examples would be the evolution of the doctrine of eminent domain, and Environmental Protection Agency regulations. The idea that the government can take private property from one person and give it to another to increase the tax base for a government entity, would not have been tolerated fifty years ago. Now this is considered legal and constitutional by some judges, governments, and citizens. It is a major step toward Marxism. In addition, a government agency, the EPA, is now allowed to accuse, adjudicate, and declare punishment on a private person for what that person does on his property simply because a government bureaucrat determines some regulation is violated - a regulation that was written by bureaucrats and never passed by elected officials. These examples are clearly the state controlling private property.

In addition to these examples, we are seeing the takeover of the financial and credit markets by the state. Marx emphasized this tool for arriving at his ideal. The control of the financial and credit markets by the state is one of the most important tools to employ in the transition to Marxism. Through these controls, the state can regulate Capitalists, not only the banker Capitalists but also the business owner. Through regulation and control of these markets, the state has dictated to the private lender to whom and how his capital should be leant. We saw this with the red-lining rules forced on bankers in the 1960's and 70's and with the rules recently imposed on lenders granting home loans. Lenders still have dictatorial regulations telling them to whom they must lend capital. Lenders are forced to make loans, regardless of collateral or borrower worthiness. This social engineering results in redistribution of assets throughout society as determined by the state and not by good business sense of the Capitalist. These demands on the financial industry have grown more and more egregious, with the most recent intrusion being the most blatant, the Dodd Frank law.

The assault on income redistribution through taxation will be continuous. The argument of the rich paying their fair share has been a rallying cry of the Progressives, Leftists, and Liberals since early history. The cry is often and loud, and when the question of what is fair is asked, the answer is always the same. That answer, is what they are now paying is not fair. The definition of fairness as seen by the Progressive, Liberals, and Leftists was given to us by Marx. He explained, that fair is when all people are receiving according to their needs and not their ability. This is why the Progressives, Liberals, and Leftists cannot give now, or ever will, give, a definitive answer to the question of what fair is.

It is important that we do not just dismiss this program put forth by Marx and promulgated by the Progressives, Liberals and Leftists as all bad, and should be totally disregarded. It is important that we note that Marx was not a monster in the likeness of Lenin, Stalin, or Mao. No record indicates he ever ordered anybody be imprisoned or killed. He did, in fact, fight for, and help bring about, child labor laws in England. He also helped bring attention to, and change in, other labor conditions that needed changing, as the society was in the throes of the change to an industrialized society.

The real aspect of the Marxist system that must be discussed in addition to its positives and negatives, is, has it and can it ever work. The Marx system has not been tried on any small experimental scales of which I am aware. Socialists established smaller experimental societies. These were somewhat common in France in the late 19th Century. Also in the mid 19th Century, Robert Owen attempted to establish a Socialist community in Indiana in the United States. As in other Socialist communities, Owen had the belief that human nature – good or bad – was a product of their environment. When people were treated in what he determined was a good and just system, they would be good and just. None of these experiments lasted for any length of time.

The experiment most closely associated with the Marx name would be the Soviet Union. Lenin was a student of Marxism. His name is commonly used with Marx to describe the system he established in Russia and, later, expanded to what was called the Soviet Union. Lenin did try to use principles taught by Marx. For instance, he insisted that the agricultural program be completely Marxist-based, despite objections from Leon Trotsky. Lenin's program had the state confiscate or collect one hundred percent of the production of the farmer. The farmer would then receive what the state determined to be his fair share. Each year, total production dropped under this arrangement. Production did not start to recover until Lenin allowed the farmer to retain half of his production for his own use and profit, and the state then took the other half. This was the program Trotsky had originally suggested, but refused by Lenin, because Lenin said it had Capitalistic elements. It did.

Marx would not have recognized the Soviet experiment, or any other experiment which has been tested under his name. It is safe to assume that he would have strongly opposed these systems. We must remember that the core of the Marxist system is that no class differences exist. Economic and political equality must exist for all. It is true that these systems used, and use, the centralized governmental control approach for both social and economic policies. This is the approach Marxism, Progressives, Liberals and Leftists advocate. A two class system, however, was not eliminated, but expanded under the Soviet Union experiment. The difference was that the new system had a party, or government bureaucrat class, that became the oppressor in place of the previous oppressor. For instance, in the case of Russia, this meant substituting one authoritarian government and oppressing class (the Czar) for another (the Party). In the United States, it is substituting a centralized system controlled by bureaucrats and academics, for a decentralized system using the concept of entrepreneurs and private business, with the belief that risk can bring rewards or failure.

Ms. West asked Biden if Obama was a Marxist. He refused to answer this question, either because he did not understand the question, or he did not want to answer it. Perhaps Ms. West should have asked the following questions:

Does Obama believe in a heavy progressive graduated income tax?

Does Obama believe in heavy death taxes?

Does Obama believe in centralized government with strict environmental and consumer controls?

Does Obama believe in federal control of communications and transportation?

Does Obama believe in federal regulation and control over banks, other financial institutions, and private companies?

Does Obama believe in federal regulation dictating to whom credit should be granted and under what terms and conditions?

Does Obama believe labor should be unionized and these unions should have say in management?

Does Obama believe in confiscation of private property for the greater good of the community?

Does Obama believe the rights of the community supersede the rights of the individual?

These are the questions all Americans should be asking themselves, their current elected representatives, and any aspirant for elected office. These are the differences between the Marxist way of life and the Capitalistic way of life.

 Most importantly, Obama must define what the FUNDAMENTAL TRANSFORMATION he advocates and seeks really means. The answer must be judged based on actions and not words. Do we really seek this FUNDAMENTAL TRANSFORMATION?

Bibliography

Balibar, Etienne "The Philosophy of Marx"
Verso 1995

Berlin, Isaiah "Karl Marx" Oxford University
Press 1966

D'amato, Paul "The Meaning of Marxism"
Haymarket Books 2006

Gabriel, Mary "Love and Capital" Little Brown
and Company 2011

Hunt, Tristram "Marx's General The
Revolutionary Life of Friedrich Engels
Metropolitan Books 2009

Marx, Karl and Engels, Friedrich "The Communist
Manifesto" Penguin Books

Tucker, Robert C. Editor "The Marx-Engels
Reader"
W. W. Norton & Company

Wheen, Francis "Marx's Das Kapital" Grove Press

Wheen, Francis "Karl Marx A Life" W. W. Norton &
Company

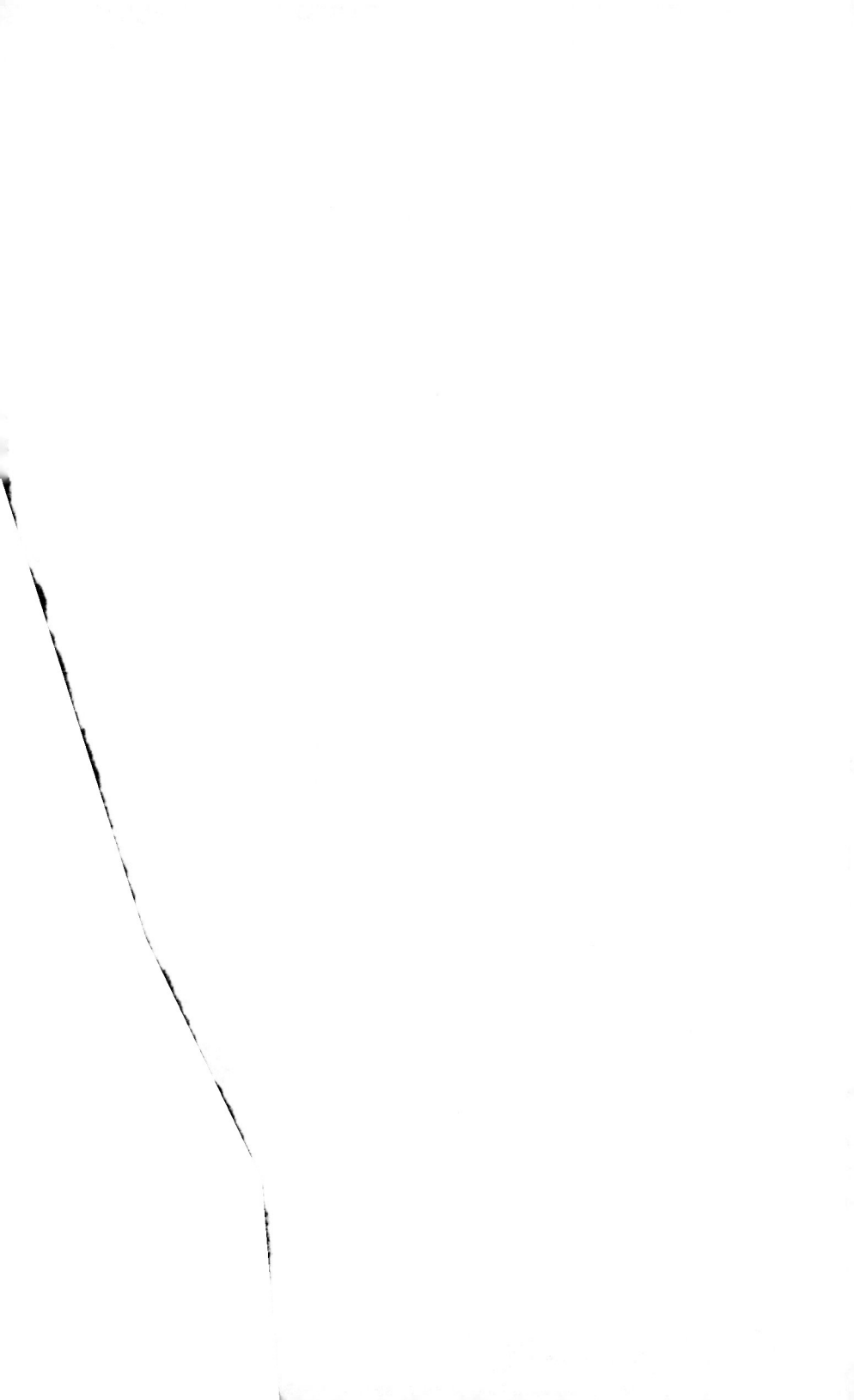